A KNIGHT IN THE FOREST

Written and Illustrated by Dan Foote

Equipping Kids for Life!
faithkids.com

Faith Parenting Guide

Ages 4-7

Humility

A Faith Parenting Guide
is found on page 32.

Faith Kids® is an imprint of
Cook Communications Ministries, Colorado Springs, CO 80918
Cook Communications, Paris, Ontario
Kingsway Communications, Eastbourne, England

A KNIGHT IN THE FOREST
©2002 by Dan Foote

First printing, 2002
Printed in Singapore

1 2 3 4 5 6 7 8 9 10 Printing/Year 06 05 04 03 02

Edited by: Mary McNeil
Cover & Interior Design: Dana Sherrer, iDesignEtc.

ISBN: 0-78143-796-2

　　　Library of Congress Cataloging-in-Publication Data

Foote, Dan.
  A knight in the forest / written and illustrated by Dan Foote.
        p. cm.
Summary: More than anything, Ben wants to be a knight and when he enters the forbidden forest alone, he learns what it takes to become a servant of the King.
  ISBN 0-7814-3796-2
  [1. Christian life--Fiction. 2. Conduct of life--Fiction. 3. Knights and knighthood--Fiction.] I. Title.
  PZ7 .F7435 Kn 2002
  [E]--dc21   2001004516

To Mom and Dad Foote and Hysell...
For the love you showed by leading us to the "full armor of God"
and the courage to stand beside us as we made it our own.

enjamin lived in the shadow of the King's castle. Magical things happened every day; knights in shining armor traveled by his house regularly, and strange creatures were commonplace. Ben and his dog, Jake, loved to play near the edge of the forbidden forest. He'd heard plenty of stories about mean giants and huge bears, and everybody who saw him playing told him to stay out of the forest.

en knew that the King's knights were the only ones who dared enter the forbidden forest. He knew that whatever they did in there called not only for courage, but for lots of practice. The castle courtyard was always filled with galloping horses, flying banners, and clashing swords. Ben could hear the knights practicing for hours; and he loved to listen to the pledge they made each time they gathered at the Round Table: *Do justly. Love mercy. Walk humbly with your King.* "I could do that!" Ben told Jake.

Ben wanted to be a knight more than anything. One day he decided to make his dream come true. He gathered up everything a knight could possibly need: an old cast-iron kettle for a helmet, a rusty stove pipe for a breastplate, and the well cover for a shield. After finding a broken piece of the backyard fence for his sword, Ben was suited and ready for battle.

old still, Jake!" Ben shouted as he jumped on the little dog's back. Jake strained from the weight. Thrusting his sword into the air Ben called out, "Do justly! Love mercy! Walk humbly with your King!" Jake's legs began to quiver, but Ben was too proud of himself to notice until . . . Crash! Armor flew everywhere, and by the time Ben picked himself up out of the dirt, Jake had run off.

en wandered toward the forbidden forest, his sword held boldly before him. "I am a great knight!" he hollered. He stood at the edge of the forest and stared in. *It can't hurt to take just one step in, can it?* But one step led to another, and soon Ben was deep in the forest.

"Who goes there?" a deep voice boomed.

Ben turned, but all he could see was

the inside of the kettle.

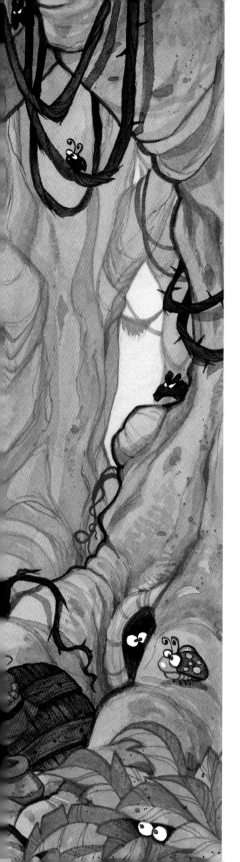

hen Ben finally got the kettle off his head, he couldn't believe his eyes. Standing before him was a giant every bit as big as the trees that surrounded him. The giant asked, "Are you a knight?" Ben turned to run, but a vine tripped him. The giant stepped closer. "They say knights are bad." Ben couldn't budge. "They say knights don't do what's right." Ben covered his face but shouted into his hands, "The King's knights are good. They do what's right!"

he giant leaned down and picked Ben high off the ground. "Don't be scared, little knight." Shaking, Ben wriggled around to look at the giant—and saw a great big toothless grin covering the giant's face. "My name's Timothy," said the giant. "Hi, Timothy"—Ben sighed in relief—"I'm Ben." But Timothy's smile suddenly faded. "Ben, I'm lost. Do you know the way out of the forest?" Benjamin nodded his head. "You bet I do. Put me down and I'll show you."

s the new friends started walking, something strange happened. The closer Ben and Timothy got to the edge of the forest, the more the thorns and briars seemed to reach out and grab Timothy. Soon he was stuck like a piece of gum in your hair. Ben tried to cut his friend free, but the wooden sword was useless. "See! Knights are bad!" Timothy shouted. Instantly the vines released him, and with a sad backward glance, Timothy walked back into the heart of the forest.

Ben left the forbidden forest in tears. *I can't do anything by myself. I should never have gone into the forest.* As he wiped away a tear, he noticed a man walking beside him. The man smiled. "Are you one of the King's knights?" Ben looked down sadly and shook his head. "Well, I say you are," the man said warmly. Ben stopped and looked more closely at the man. It was the King himself!

The King leaned over and wiped away Ben's tears. "You have done *justly* by wanting to serve me," the King said. "You have shown *mercy* by trying to free that poor giant from the forest. And now, Benjamin, you walk *humbly* by my side. You now understand what it really means to be my knight." Ben's shame melted away with each loving word. "All you need," the King told him, "is some real armor."

Filled with love and awe, Ben knelt before the King. He felt the King's heavy sword gently touch his head—and a warm burst of light spread through him. Ben's play armor transformed into real armor, beautiful and shiny, and the King pulled Ben to his feet. "Now, go back to Timothy," the King said softly, "and remember that I am always with you." The King disappeared.

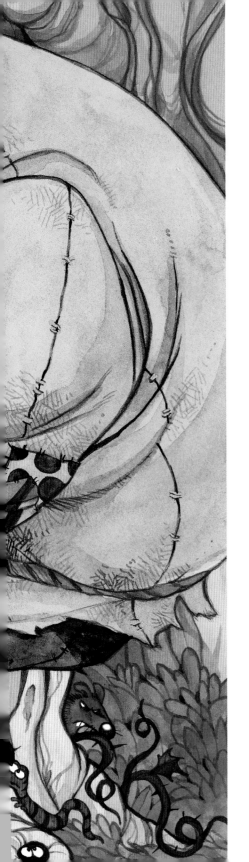

en didn't hesitate. He ran back into the forest. "Did you think I left you?" Ben called to Timothy with a laugh. The giant turned around in surprise. "Come on, Timothy! Now I know how to get you out of here." The giant's eyes grew round. "The only way for you to leave the forest," Ben declared, "is to become a knight. Do you want to be one of the King's knights, too?" Timothy smiled that toothless grin and nodded "yes"—and he too received the beautiful shining armor.

en and Timothy made their way back to the kingdom. It grew darker with each footstep and the wind blew heavy in the trees above. But Ben wasn't afraid. He knew the King was with him. "Ben! I'm stuck!" Timothy yelled out. Once again, the thorns and briars had pinned the giant to a tree. Only this time, Timothy had a sword! He raised it high above his head and, with one fell swoop, cut himself free!

The entire kingdom—including Ben's father and trusty Jake—was waiting in celebration as Ben and Timothy stepped from the forbidden forest. Timothy smiled that toothless grin. Ben smiled too because he knew he would soon join the other knights on many adventures, keeping their pledge to *Do justly; Love mercy; Walk humbly with your King.*

Faith Parenting Guide

Ages 4-7

Humility

A Knight in the Forest

Life Issue: I want my children to walk with God.

Help your children to nurture a healthy sense of humility before God in the following ways:

Sight: Go to a park with your children and watch how dogs act toward good masters. Their wagging tails and happy barks indicate their complete love and trust in the master. Talk about how we can love and trust our God so much more—because we have the very best Master of all.

Sound: Often when we pray, we tell God how much we love him, we thank him for the good things he gives us, we ask for blessings, we say sorry for doing things wrong—and these are all proper things to pray about. But this time when you pray with your children, simply be still and listen. Maybe God wants to say something to you.

Touch: *A Knight in the Forest* is based on the Bible verse Micah 6:8: "What does the Lord require of you? To act justly and to love mercy and to walk humbly with your God." Help your children understand humility by role playing accepting a compliment. For example, if someone tells your child he or she made a beautiful drawing, the child's response would be "thank you" rather than "I know" or "no, it's not."